The Spirit of Cricket

WISDEN

The Spirit of Cricket

KENSINGTON WEST PRODUCTIONS
HEXHAM ENGLAND

Kensington West Productions Ltd
5 Cattle Market, Hexham, Northumberland NE46 1NJ
Tel: (01434) 609933, Fax: (01434) 600066/600422
e mail: kwp@kensingtonwest.demon.co.uk
web site: www.kensingtonwest.demon.co.uk

Photographs by	**Designed by**
Allsport	Nick Ridley
Features	**Production**
Frank Keating	Mark Scandle
Editor	**Origination by**
Helen Parker	Pre-Press Ltd, Hong Kong
Picture Editor	**Printing by**
Mark Goldsmith	Liang Yu Printing Factory, Hong Kong

Frontispiece: Mark Butcher chases after the ball as Greg Blewett and Matthew Elliott cross for a quick single during the 2nd Ashes Test at Lord's, 1997. **Photograph:** Adrian Murrell. **Title Page:** Darren Gough runs out Jason Gillespie's runner, Michael Bevan during the 1st Test at Edgbaston, 1997. **Photograph:** Clive Mason. **Facing:** Jonty Rhodes crashes into the stumps as Damien Fleming attempts to run him out. **Photograph:** Graham Chadwick. **Acknowledgments:** David Gower dodges a short delivery from India's Chetan Sharma. **Photograph:** Adrian Murrell. **Facing:** Mark Taylor attempting a spectacular stop. **Photograph:** Shaun Botterill. **Introduction:** (top) England slip fielders, 2nd Ashes Test, Lord's, 1981. **Photograph:** Adrian Murrell. (bottom) Umpires examining the ball. **Photograph:** Allsport.

Contents

Introduction

The spirit of cricket is a notably elusive one. Most games are recognisably the same wherever they are being played: a game of football is a game of football; a round of golf is a round of golf.

A cricket match might comprise a man wearing a lime-green pyjama suit rushing in under floodlights to hurl a leather projectile at an armoured and helmeted figure 20 yards away, perhaps in scarlet or powder blue, roared on by thirty, fifty, maybe a hundred thousand partisans. The same pyjama-suited figures might find themselves, only a few days later, playing in an English county match, wearing whites, watched spasmodically by thirty, fifty, maybe a hundred dozy folk in deckchairs. That's all professional cricket.

When it's played for fun, the spirit might be embodied by 22 beautifully turned-out public schoolboys playing with top-of-the-range, carefully calibrated bats on a neatly mown square in the Home Counties under the tutelage of an elderly master, benign until he sees the merest smidgin of dissent about his rulings.

But that spirit is also embodied (these days more effectively embodied) on the waste ground of the sub-continent, where ragged, yelling, street kids use rough lumps of wood to whack misshapen balls into the next group of ragged street kids.

From village green to Vishakhapatnam, no other game has so many contrasting moods; this book reflects many of them.

Matthew Engel
Editor, Wisden Cricketers' Almanack

The Bat and the Ball

And so it came to pass

My father knew nothing of cricket. But in 1947 he took me to my first cricket match, and for a couple of hours we watched our county's heroes play Middlesex at Gloucester. I was nine, and I was entranced. My father knew nothing of cricket, but the following year on holiday on the Hampshire coast, he took me to Hambledon, the birthplace of the game. I was ten, and I was hooked.

The first great cricket club was founded on that bare south country pasture above the Meon Valley. On that downland paddock of spring turf, two centuries before, shepherds had watched their flocks cropping the grass as short as a convict's hairdo. And at the end of the day, in fraternal reverie those men and boys would play at bat and ball in ancient custom, defending with their crook, or 'crick' the shepherd's three-pronged movable gate, or 'wicket'. Lower down in the woodland valleys, just as readily, foresters in a clearing might have chopped down a tree and, here, its stump would be the target for the batsman to protect, the bowler to assail.

Alongside Hambledon's Common there stood an inn. It became known as The Bat and Ball. From there they began to write and codify the 'laws' of this pastime - the length of a 'pitch', for instance, was to be that of a forester's chain (22 yards), the height of the 'wicket' gate 22 inches, its width half that at 11 inches . . . and 11 men, if possible, would play on each side. The game thus formalised was to spread like a blaze into the neighbouring agricultural counties, thence through the village greens to the newly industrialised north and midlands where young artisans took to it with a will - and so, in no time, did schools and universities, and the Services.

Yeoman farmers sponsored teams, so did wealthy landowners, and soon enough, large crowds gathered to watch the game played on green spaces in the capital itself, like the Artillery Ground in Finsbury and Thomas Lord's Ground at Marylebone. In Hampshire, the first landlord of The Bat and Ball Inn had been Richard Nyren, a champion player. In 1833, his son John published the game's first lasting chronicle *Cricketers of my Time*. 'Little Hambledon against All England was the proud boast of the Hampshire men,' he wrote. And so it came to pass. Nyren Jnr. died, at 73, in June 1837, precisely a century before I was born. It was the same year the 18-year old Victoria ascended to the English throne. Eleven midsummers later, William Gilbert Grace was born near Bristol on July 18, 1848 - the very same week, plus 100 years, that I first set eyes on the grazing sheep at Hambledon. And exactly half a century on from then, by fluke, I took my own small son to The Bat and Ball Inn at Hambledon. Sheep still nibbled, busy and oblivious, as the village cricketers, out in the middle, flickered to and fro ... and from the pub, as the poet Edmund Blunden had it,

> ' . . . they watched their sons
> Playing till too dark to see,
> As their fathers watched them once
> As my father once watched me.'

The Carlton & United One-Day series in Australia 1999.
Exit Arjuna Ranatunga

(opposite) Children playing in Pakista

Chapter One

Photograph: Shaun Botterill

Grass Roots and Early Years

(above) A young cricketer in Pakistan.

Photograph: Clive Mason

Craft Versed Giants

The wise innocents of cricket

Dr Grace played for Gloucestershire. He was to become almost as famed as the Queen-Empress herself, certainly more recognisable around the Empire than Prime Ministers Disraeli or Gladstone. Dr Grace created modern cricket. He was sport's inaugural superstar. He scored his first century in 1864, his last in 1908. In all cricket he scored 100,000 runs, took well over 7,000 wickets and held 1,500 catches. They called him The Champion. He had trod, and only two-score years before, the very same Gloucester field I was first taken to watch cricket by my father in 1947.

The Gloucestershire cricketers who succeeded Grace were the giants of my youth. Giants they remain. Even when my boyhood's callow, eyes-wide idol worship had been replaced - as, in time, it was in many cases, with a fondly warm man-to-man friendship, I am still in awe of these cigarette-card heroes of my youth. There was music in the names of these wise innocents when I first heard them long ago; and a valorous chivalry in their deeds. Most of them are dead now. A half-century on, the eyes (like those of all really good cricketers, have you noticed?) of those still alive remain piercing bright and steady-gazed; their faces and forearms still burnished with a sun-brown wash which tells of those countless midsummers in the open air. The gnarled and knobbly twisted knuckles of their thumbs and fingers are proof and testament to the exacting trade and craft for which I loved them: a skill-based craft for sure aye - and more, for it was one which from time to time allowed them to be uplifted into brief but very genuine realms of creative invention and authentic artistry. Some know-all once said that the process of maturity into adulthood reduced giants to man-size. Not so with the officers and foot-sloggers - especially not the foot-sloggers - who strode the green turf of my favourite cricketing fields of childhood.

If nothing else, these good men taught us urchins pride - for with all our youthful fibre, oh boy, what pride we had in them. I'll give you a half-dozen of my puppyhood who played for England, some of them enchanting vast throngs of many thousands in grandiose concrete arenas in cities across the seas and far from distant, pastoral, glorious Gloucestershire: Barnett, Emmett, Graveney, Milton, Cook, and Goddard. Just as most every boy still can recite his own particular litany from his particular own county . . .

(above) A young Zimbabwean in a classic spinner's action.

A. STEWART					BATSMAN		G. WHITALL		
M. ATHERTON					M. ABRAMS	6	M. RANCHOD	0	20
N. HUSSAIN					BATSMAN		H. STREAK	67	175
A. CADDICK	16	5	36	1			W. JAMES	7	85
D. GOUGH	15	2	47	2	TOTAL	198			
P. TUFNELL	16	3	59		WKTS	4			
G. THORPE	3		6		ZIM 1ST INN	188			
R. CROFT	15	4	34	1	2ND INN				
J. CRAWLEY					VISIT 1ST INN	334			
N. KNIGHT					2ND INN	230	OVERS		
							EXTRAS		
							R. TIFFIN	C. CO	

Children's cricket during the England tour of Zimbabwe in December 1996.

Photograph: Stu Forster

Jack Russell with a young local enthusiast during the England tour of the West Indies in 1990.

Photograph: Adrian Murrell

Youngsters play cricket during the England tour of Zimbabwe in February 1999.

Photograph: Laurence Griffiths

Photograph: Graham Chadwick

Children playing cricket during the England 'A' tour of Sri Lanka in 1998.

The Spirit of Cricket 13

Photograph: Laurence Griffiths

(left) A children's match in Jamaica from the England tour of the West Indies, January 1998.

(below) Star batsman Martin Speight (who later played for Sussex and Durham) is out.
Sussex Colts Under-11s, May 1979.

Photograph: Adrian Murrell

Children at play during the Worcestershire v. India match at New Road, Worcester in May 1996.

Photograph: Graham Chadwick

Village cricket: Bramley v Sunbury Village at Bramley in Surrey, July 1996.

Village cricket.

Photograph: Allsport

Village cricket: Brighton, Sussex.

Village cricket: Ockley in Surrey, July 1995.

Yorkshire v Durham in the Scarborough Cricket Festival 1992.

(opposite) England and Australia practising slip catching
prior to the Third Test at the Adelaide Oval.

Chapter Two

Photograph: Graham Chadwick

Practice makes Perfect

(left) Noisy net practice during the England tour of India in 1993.

(right) The Australian team train before the Second Test v. England at the Waca, Perth, November 1998.

Photograph: Graham Chadwick

(above) Mike Atherton (England) in the nets during the 1997
tour of New Zealand.

(right) Nick Knight (England) warms up.
Carlton & United One-Day series, January 1999.

Photograph: Clive Mason

Photograph: Ben Radford

Graham Gooch batting in the nets before the First Test at Calcutta. England tour of India, 1993.

Photograph: Shaun Botterill

England in the nets...

before the Lord's Test against Sri Lanka in 1991.

before the Third Test v Australia at the Adelaide Oval in December 1998.

Photograph: Laurence Griffiths

Photograph: Ben Radford

Allan Border sharpens up before the First One-Day match against England at Old Trafford, May 1993.

Photograph: Mark Thompson

Shaun Pollock buries one in the net.
Combined Universities v Warwickshire in The Parks, Oxford, April 1996.

Photograph: Ben Radford

(left) Graham Gooch prior to the Third Test against India at Bombay, February 1993.

(below) Net practice.

Photograph: Anton Want

(left) Kepler Wessels, captain of South Africa during their tour of Australia, December 1993.

Photograph: Ben Radford

Photograph: Clive Mason

(right) Nasser Hussain pads up during the Carlton & United One-Day series in Australia, January 1999.

Photograph: Ben Radford

Photograph: Laurence Griffiths

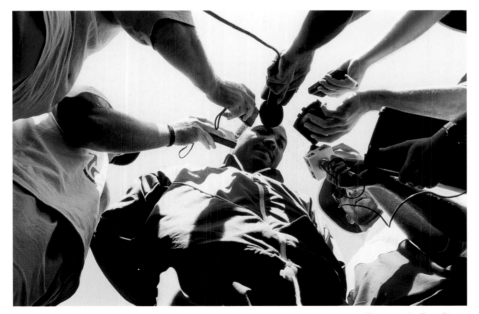

Photograph: Tom Shaw

Facing the Cameras

(above left) Allan Border, Pakistan v. Australia Third Test at Karachi, October 1998.

(above right) Brian Lara at Edgbaston during a Warwickshire photocall, 1998.

(below left) West Indies captain Brian Lara talks to the press before the Second Test against Australia at Sabina Park, Jamaica in March 1999.

Waqar Younis (Pakistan) during his warm-up exercises.
England v. Pakistan, Third Test at The Oval, August 1996.

Groundstaff prepare the wicket before the World Cup match between the United Arab Emirates and England at Peshawar, February 1996.

Baking in the sun.

Photograph: Ben Radford

The groundstaff before the Second Test between Pakistan and Australia, October 1998.

West Indies warm up before the First Test against England at Headingley in June 1991.

Photograph: Adrian Murrell

Australia, ready to roll during net practice at Lord's, Ashes series 1997.

Photograph: Adrian Murrell

A high-powered drinks cart!
Sri Lanka v. India at Ahmedabad during the
Nehru Cup in 1989.

Photograph: Adrian Murrell

Changing the Culture

Undeniably the very best

The immensity of Grace introduced cricket to the wider world. In spirit and often in person, he took the game to the furthest outposts of Victoria's Empire. Having established cricket as a national institution, he now turned it into a global one. For this still practising Bristol doctor, in his sporting pomp no sun was too hot for him, no day too long . . . Grace's last first-class match at Lord's was in April 1908. He was 60 that July. A month later he played his last match at London's other arena of grandeur, The Oval at Kennington. He scored 33 and took three wickets. It was August 20.

Just seven days later on the other side of the world, at Cootamundra near Bowral in New South Wales, was born to an upcountry carpenter and his wife a son. The Bradmans named him Donald George. The boy's early passion was for tennis. He left school at 14 and became an estate agent's clerk in Bowral. In 1925, the Bowral cricket club asked the small lad with the ledger-writer's neat handwriting if he would like to be their match secretary as well as play for them in the Berrima District League. He did, and in the 1925-26 season, he batted 23 times at an astonishing average of 94.14. The following November, just 18, he travelled the 82-mile journey north-east to the capital by train with his father to take part in a one-day boys' trial match at the Sydney Cricket Ground. On November 11, 1926, the Sydney Morning Herald reported in a single downpage paragraph: 'Probables: 302 for nine (AF Kippax 58, AA Jackson 53). Possibles: 237 (DG Bradman 37 not out). . .

Bradman showed supreme confidence, and the further he went the better he shaped. He was one of the few batsmen in the game to leave his crease to the slow deliveries. He would retire from cricket in 1948, just a month after WG's centenary. Bradman took his curtain call at The Oval against England. He walked to that wicket needing just four runs to average 100. He was bowled for nought. So he ended with a Test match batting average of 99.94. His average in all first-class cricket was 95.14.

Bradman's relentless batting made him undeniably better than even Grace had been. In so doing he changed the very culture of his new and callow country. Said the Nobel-winning Australian author Thomas Keneally: 'As late as the 1950s, the curriculum in Australian schools was identical to that of England. Poetry cut out at Tennyson. The only history was European history. When we learned of literary figures, we learned of Englishmen. No Australian had written *Paradise Lost*. But Bradman had made 100 before lunch at Lord's.'

Darren Gough (England) during net practice
in Bulawayo, December 1996.

(left) Allan Border and Ian Botham set the scene for Sky TV before the Fourth Test between Australia and England at Melbourne.

The Third Test, Pakistan v. Australia at Karachi, October 1998.
(top right) Captains Aamir Sohail and Mark Taylor decide the toss with match referee Peter van der Merwe.

(bottom right) Peter van der Merwe checks the width of a bat.

An historic moment: Clive Rice, captain of South Africa, in the nets before the first one-day match against India at Calcutta, November 1991.
South Africa's first match after returning to the international cricket scene.

(opposite) Overenthusiastic West Indian supporters celebrate Lara's double-hundred.

Chapter Three

Photograph: Tom Shaw

For the Love of the Game

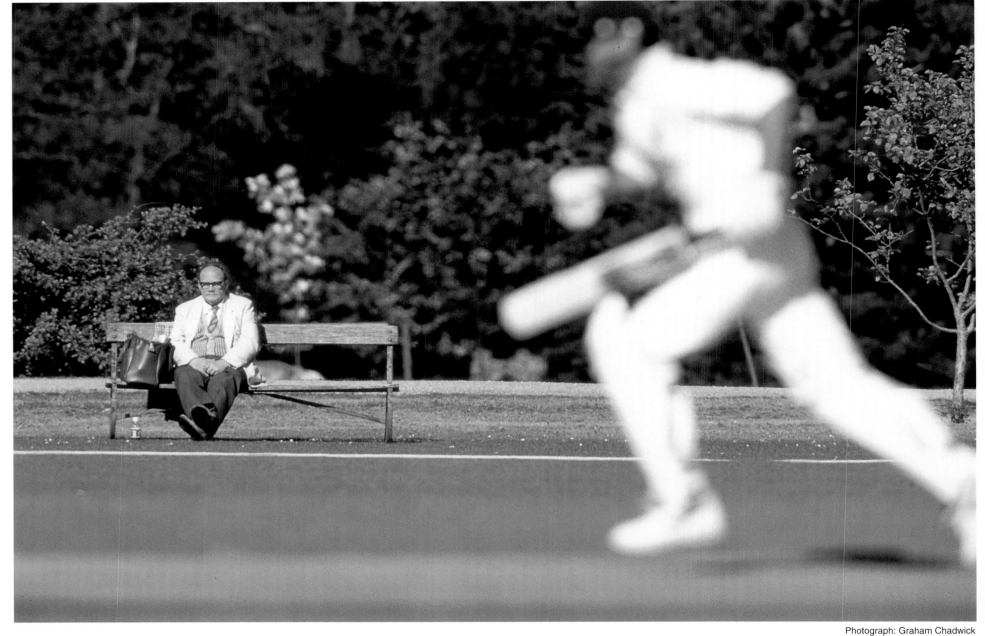

Photograph: Graham Chadwick

The Crowd in The Parks
Graeme Hick in action for Worcestershire against Oxford University in 1997.

A village match spectator.

Enjoying cricket at Lord's during the Second Test, England against the West Indies in June 1991.

Crowds at the final of the Women's World Cup in India, 1997.

Merv Hughes loosens up the crowd during the first final of the World Series at the Melbourne Cricket Ground in January 1989.

Photograph: Stu Forster

The England team acknowledge the Barmy Army.
Fifth Test, Australia v. England at the Sydney
Cricket Ground, January 1999.

Pakistan supporters during the World Cup match between Pakistan and Scotland
at The Riverside, Chester-le-Street, Co. Durham, England in May 1999.

Photograph: Laurence Griffiths

The Coca-Cola Cup at Sharjah in April 1999.

India v. South Africa, the Third One-Day match at New Delhi in November 1991.

Photograph: Shaun Botterill

Local support for John Emburey in Faisalabad. Pakistan 'A' against England 'A', Second One-Day match.

Photograph: Ben Ra

A South African supporters' band keeps
the crowd entertained.
South Africa v. England, Fourth Test at
Port Elizabeth, December 1995.

The cool fans watch from the pool.
West Indies v. Australia, First Test at the Queen's Park
Oval, Port-of-Spain, Trinidad in March 1999.

Photograph: Ross Kinnaird

The Bangladesh fans invade the pitch after the victory over Pakistan in the World Cup at Northampton, England in May 1999.

The crowd welcomes the Australian team home to Melbourne after winning the World Cup in June 1999.

Allan Lamb's ovation after his century during the Fourth Test, West Indies v. England in Barbados, April 1990.

Photograph: Rob Cianflone

Photograph: Ben Radford

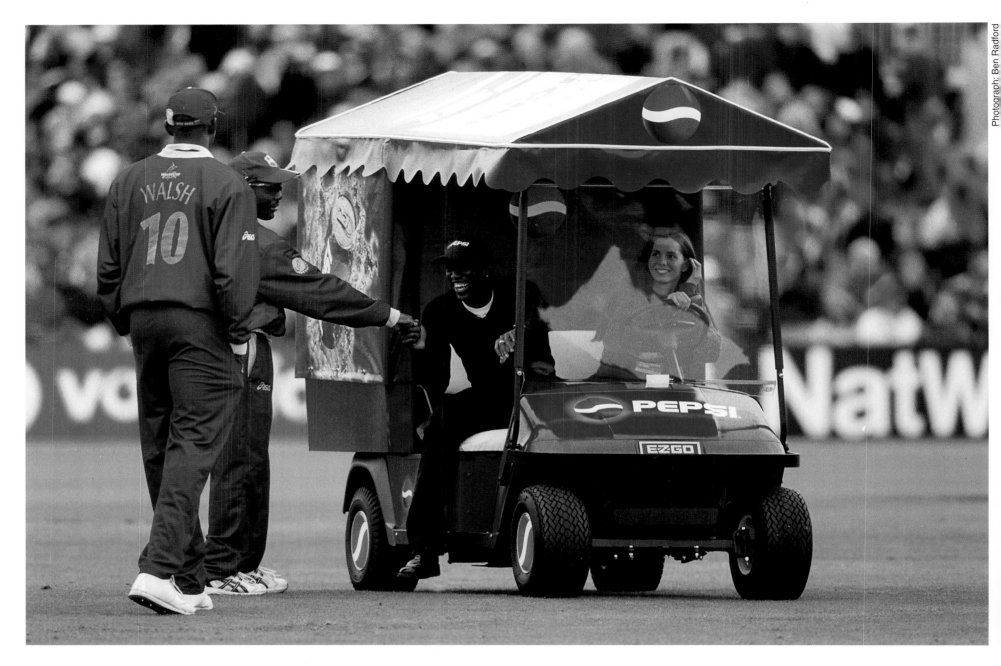

Manchester United star Dwight Yorke brings on the drinks.
West Indies v. Australia at Old Trafford, England during the World Cup, May 1999.

(opposite) South Africa celebrate victory
against Australia in the First Test at
Johannesburg, March 1994.

Chapter Four

When the Match Turns

Photograph: Clive Mason

England's Phil Tufnell in Irish Dancing mood. England v. Australia, Sixth Test at The Oval in August 1997.

The following day Tufnell leads the celebrations as England win the Sixth Test.

Lance Klusener (South Africa) takes the wicket of Alpesh Vadher (Kenya) caught and bowled, in their World Cup match at Amstelveen in Holland, May 1999.

Brendon Julian (Australia) catches John Crawley (England) in the Carlton & United One-Day series in Australia, January 1999.

Photograph: Clive Mason

England's Alec Stewart takes the long walk back to the pavilion. Third Test, West Indies v. England in Trinidad, February 1998.

Photograph: Adrian Murrell

Alec Stewart in a better mood during the Third Test against South Africa at Old Trafford in June 1998.

Shoaib Akhtar of Pakistan appeals against the West Indies in the World Cup, Bristol, England, May 1999.

Photograph: Clive Mason

Shoaib Akhtar takes the wicket of Steve Waugh during the World Cup match between Pakistan and Australia at Headingley, May 1999.

Photograph: Ben Radford

England captain Mike Atherton celebrates the fall of another wicket as England win the Sixth Test against Australia at The Oval in August 1997.

Photograph: Shaun Botterill

The jubilant West Indies team celebrate victory over South Africa. This was South Africa's first Test match after returning to international competition. April 1992.

Photograph: Laurence Griffiths

More cause for West Indies celebration, England's Nasser Hussain out LBW to a shooter delivery in the Third Test in Trinidad in February 1998.

Photograph: Shaun Botterill

They are the Masters Now

The old order changes

Other worlds were just as readily conquered, and other poets logged their paeans to cricket. The Indian subcontinent took to their imperial master's game with a passion. Princes played cricket and so did paupers.

Indian Salman Rushdie remembers a Bombay childhood spent 'listening to Vijay Hazare scoring crackling centuries on a crackling wireless.' India first beat England at cricket in 1951. The Pakistani author Tariq Ali revels still in the memory of 'envy of the apparently carefree life of the street children who played cricket the whole day long during the idyllic winter months from November till March.' Pakistan first beat England at cricket in 1954. My own Gloucestershire laureate Laurie Lee boasted of how his Uncle Sid, a Boer War private in the British Army, helped, with his 'catapulting hitting' and his 'gale-force bowling', teach the Dutch South Africans on the sweltering Veld what he had learned 'on the hillocks and molehills' of his beloved homeland of Sheepscombe. The West Indian radical-philosopher CLR James hoorayed cricket as a metaphor for the Empire and claimed the game had fuelled, in turn, the democratic revolutions of Australia, New Zealand, the Subcontinent, and the Caribbean. In the nineteenth century, when Grace was batting at home - he toured Australia and the United States at cricket, but never the Caribbean - the game had been the instrument of colonial exclusion used by the elite European 'masters' society to distance and detach itself from the servile black majority.

By the 1930s such a regime and culture came under fire and once the West Indian black sides began to humble their masters at the game - England were first beaten in 1950, and at Lord's of all places - cricket became hinged irrevocably to the progress of anticolonial reforms and the movement towards independence and nation building. James was from Trinidad. So was Learie Constantine, still considered the game's greatest fieldsman. Brian Lara was from Trinidad: at the century's end, his innings of 375 in a Test, and 501 in a first-class match, remain unsurpassed in history. From the tiny island of Antigua had come possibly the most haughty and mercilessly destructive of any batsman, Vivian Richards. From Barbados came a batting triumvirate of utter splendour, Weekes, Worrell, and Walcott - the three Ws - as well as the most resplendent all-rounder the cricket world has seen, Garfield Sobers. By the turn of the new century, an Australian (Allan Border) had scored more Test runs than anyone before, and an Indian (Kapil Dev), taken more wickets.

West Indies celebrate success in the
Second Test against Australia in Antigua.
April 1995.

(left) Craig McDermott (Australia) takes the wicket of Sri Lanka's Asanka Gurusinha in the First Test at Perth in December 1995.

(right) Darren Gough dismisses Australia's Greg Blewett in the First Test of the Ashes series at Edgbaston, England, June 1997.

Photograph: Adrian Murrell

Ian Bishop in celebratory mood.
England v. West Indies Sixth Test at The Oval, England, August 1995.

Brian Lara (West Indies captain) claims a souvenir after his side's one-wicket victory over Australia in the Third Test in Barbados, March 1999.

Glenn McGrath is bowled by Lance Klusener for 11.
Third Test, South Africa v. Australia at Centurion Park, March 1997.

Photograph: Tertius Pickard

Allan Border (Australia) knocks the stumps over in disgust after being dismissed in a tour match against Middlesex at Lord's, May 1993.

England's Mike Atherton, bowled out in the Second Test in Trinidad, February 1998.

Australia's Geoff Lawson jumps for joy after taking the wicket of Viv Richards in the World Series, Australia v. West Indies, February 1985.

Mark Butcher is out.
Second Test, Australia v. England at the Waca, Perth, November 1998.

**The West Indies team queue to celebrate with Courtney Walsh in the Sixth Test against England
in Antigua, March 1998.**

Photograph: Clive Mason

Darren Gough gets an early bath after England win the Second Test against New Zealand at Wellington in February 1997.

Australia celebrate another wicket in the Fourth Test v. West Indies in Jamaica, May 1995.

Photograph: Shaun Botterill

(opposite) Jonty Rhodes taking y
another outstanding catc

Chapter Five

Great Moments

Don Bradman's last innings, England v. Australia at The Oval, 1948.

Bill Woodfull (Australia) ducks a ball from
Harold Larwood during the infamous Bodyline
series - England v. Australia at Brisbane, March
1933.

John Inverarity is LBW to Derek Underwood
and England clinch victory over Australia with
a few minutes to spare at The Oval in 1968.

Graham Gooch breaks his hand in the Third Test between the West Indies and England in Trinidad in 1990.

Photograph: Shaun Botterill.

Umpire Steve Bucknor seems unsure.
World Cup Super Six stage, Zimbabwe v. Pakistan at The Oval, June 1999.

Photograph: Laurence Griffiths

The score's 111, and superstitious David Shepherd can't bear to touch the ground.
England v. Sri Lanka Test at The Oval, August 1998.

It all gets to be too much.

Umpire Dickie Bird's last Test match before retirement. England v. India, Second Test at Lord's in June 1996. Photos: Adrian Murrell and Graham Chadwick

Feeling the strain in the Texaco Trophy one-day series. England v. West Indies at The Oval, May 1995.

The Best of the Best

And the baton gets handed on

A year after I first visited with my father that flat and evocative field at Hambledon alongside The Bat and Ball Inn, I went to my first Test match. It was at Manchester's Old Trafford, England versus New Zealand in a heatwave splurge in the midsummer of 1949. I was 11 years and 296 days old, and making his first appearance in England colours was, and still, the youngest ever to do so. Brian Close was aged 18 years and 149 days. He was a spare, lanky and baby-faced Yorkshire all-rounder; he sported a severe National Service short-back-and-sides haircut, and asked one of us schoolboys to hold the butt of his smoking Woodbine ciggie as he signed our autograph books behind the pavilion before play began. He took one wicket (with a full toss) and was caught for a duck at deepest square-leg off the game's boldest stroke.

Close ever since remained one of my favourite characters in a game which gloriously continues to burst with them. A quarter of a century later, now a veteran field-marshal, Close was captaining Somerset. It was 1974 and this ageing hero of mine, now 'the bald old blighter', introduced me proudly to his pupil and apprentice. The stripling was a countryman, also spare and lanky. Ian Botham bowled fast, lived faster, and smote the ball, high, wide, and handsome, and all over Wessex. Soon enough, all over the world. Again, the baton had been passed from one generation to the next. It was the year before the death of the writer, Sir Neville Cardus. He had seen WG Grace just once. But that was enough for him to tell me how 'the Doctor had played cricket with the whole man of him in full action, body, soul, heart, and wits.' And so hurrahed us who saw Botham in his pomp all through the next decade, as morning after morning the summer's sun rose for him and he went forth and trod fresh grass and sought more conquests . . . In his time, Merrie Englander Botham was to obliterate the record books, for sixers smote, or wickets taken, or catches caught. Just as, in time, his standards and marks were, or will be overtaken. It is the way of best-ever records.

It was nicely, for instance, that in 1895, on Botham's very own same folksy paddock at Taunton that Archie MacLaren had scored 424, the highest ever made till then. Never to be beaten, they said. A quarter of a century on, and the Australian Billy Ponsford did so. Then Bradman's 452 for New South Wales topped his compatriot in 1929. Thirty years on, the Pakistani maestro Hanif Mohammad made 499. Thirty-five years later, in Birmingham, came Brian Lara's 501. Likewise, the Test match mark has been bested only six times down the century: Foster for England, 287 in 1903 at Sydney; then Bradman's 334 at Leeds in 1930, Hammond's 336 not out at Auckland two years later, and Leonard Hutton's 364 at The Oval in 1938. Twenty years on and Sobers's 365 topped that by one - to post the longest wait till 1994 and the ravishing Lara's 375 against England in Antigua. What goes around comes around . . . and one day, as sure as the morning sun, even bowler Jim Laker's 19 out of a possible 20 Test match wickets will be erased from the logs of the lore.

Dickie Bird gives one of his last decisions: Jack Russell is out LBW. England v. India, Second Test at Lord's, June 1996.

Mike Atherton goes out to bat, in the Second Test against Australia at Lord's, June 1997.
This was his 42nd Test as England captain, breaking Peter May's record.

Viv Richards hooks Ian Botham for another boundary.

Viv Richards surveys the field settings during a one-day game against Australia at Melbourne, December 1986.

Allan Border (Australian captain) at Edgbaston in the Second One-Day International against England, May 1993.

Another Australian legend, Dennis Lillee, thunders in.

(left) England captain Mike Atherton leaves the field at the end of the fifth day's play after saving the Second Test against South Africa at Johannesburg, December 1995. He scored an epic 185 not out.

(below) Mike Atherton walks back from the nets in December 1994.

Photographs: Graham Chadwick

Alex Tudor displays an excellent technique on his home debut - 99 not out in the First Test England v. New Zealand at Edgbaston, July 1999.

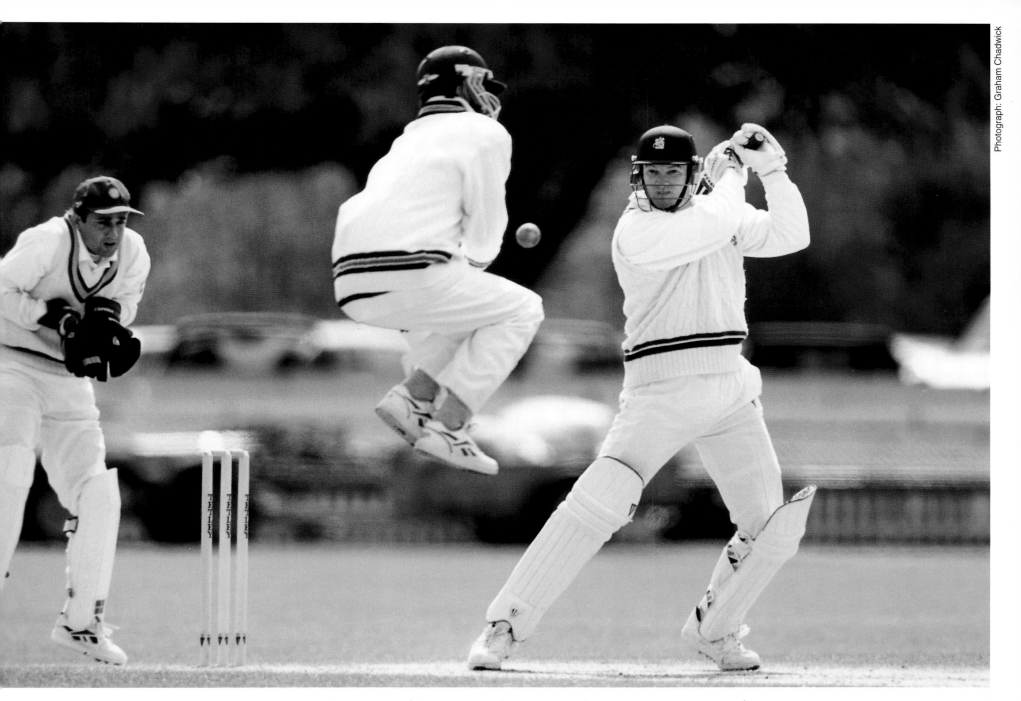

Graeme Hick on his way to 216 for Worcestershire against India at Worcester in May 1996.

(right) Ian Botham attempts a massive hook shot but falls off balance and dislodges a bail - out for 31, England v. West Indies, Fifth Test at The Oval, August 1991.

Photograph: Allsport

Dominic Cork completes a Test match hat-trick for England against the West Indies in the Fourth Test at Old Trafford, July 1995.

Photograph: Shaun Botterill

South Africa's return to the international scene.

(above) The first tour of an official England team to South Africa for nearly 30 years. England 'A' play a Transvaal Invitation XI in Alexandra against the backdrop of a shanty town, December 1993.

(right) Andrew Hudson and Gary Kirsten walk out to open the batting for South Africa in the First Test against England at Lord's in July 1994.

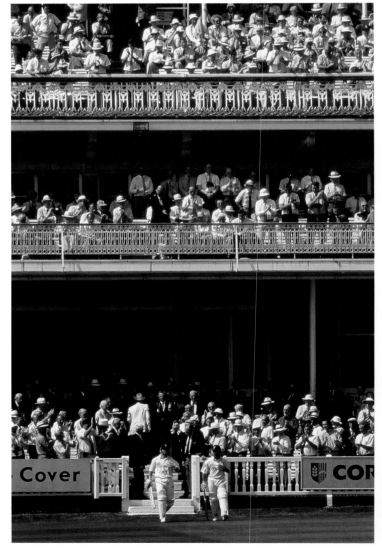

Photograph: Ben Radford

Photograph: Clive Mason

The infamous pitch at Sabina Park in Jamaica where the First Test between the West Indies and England in 1998 was abandoned on the first morning.

Photograph: Laurence Griffiths

Alec Stewart and Nasser Hussain go out to open the batting for England against Zimbabwe in the World Cup at Trent Bridge, Nottingham, May 1999.

Brian Lara during his world-record innings of 501 not out for Warwickshire against Durham at Edgbaston in June 1994.

Photograph: Ben Radford

The jubilant fans celebrate England's historic victory over Australia in the Third Test at Headingley,
England in July 1981.

South Africa's Allan Donald is run out and Australia reach the final of the World Cup. Edgbaston,
June 1999.

Australia lift the World Cup after beating Pakistan in the final at Lord's in June 1999.

Photograph: Hamish Blair

Steve Waugh and Shane Warne with the World Cup during the champions' street parade in Melbourne, June 1999.

(opposite) Headingley, during the Fifth Test. England v. South Africa, August 1998.

Chapter Six

The World of Cricket

Photograph: Clive Mason

Photograph: Craig Pren

England

Views of Lord's cricket ground, London.

Photograph: Adrian Murrell

Grounds for Acclamation

and centres of civilisation

The grandeur of cricket, in great part, is reflected in the grandeur of its grounds. The English villages of its birth remain close to cricket's heart and soul, yet so do the vast urban colosseums of Test match pretension - for what deeds were done on this day or that, remember? Who can forget - for the character of cricket's fields are invariably fashioned by the characters who inhabited them. Take any at random: Hove in Sussex, for instance, which lies next to the sea and below those southern downs where first the game was played.

Cricket at Hove has a dash, an exotic vim about it still: for there batted Ranjitsinjhi the Prince in his long-sleeved silk shirt; often in partnership with the frankly finicky but undeniably corinthian Fry; and Hove was assuredly Ted Dexter, magisterial end-of-pier ringmaster, crack of his bat like a whip. Grace was the wider world, but wherever he batted the great loner Hammond was, somehow, forever Bristol. Meanwhile the elegant Graveney was, to me, always upright Regency Cheltenham more than Worcester's honey-stoned Norman pastoral. Manchester's Old Trafford remains all MacLaren and the Tyldesleys and Washbrook, and Boycott and Leyland were far more Leeds than Lord Hawke. Mind you, think of Headingley and the Australian Bradman assails you: in four successive Test matches over 18 years at Leeds, Bradman scored 334, 304,103 and 173 not out. Nottingham's lovely, light-hearted Trent Bridge is, to me, the Gunns, the Hardstaffs, and Randall. The smiling Geordie Milburn will be forever Northampton. Gooch was Chelmsford-man personified, Cowdrey was Canterbury. If Barry Richards was far too grand for Southampton, his compatriot Mike was unquestionably Proctershire.

I saw Botham play often at Taunton, whizzing the balls over the River Tone as joyously as Sammy Woods had almost a century before. I was privileged to see Marshall bowling in, and for, Barbados, and Lillee bowl a bouncer with his wolf-like grin, in Perth. And Gavaskar score a century in Bombay. The grounds went with the men. In London, I love the jingle-jangle and jabber of The Oval, where the mighty Hobbs, and Sandham and Barrington each concentrated with an accent characteristic and Cockney. Across the river to the north, Lord's is more pontifical, all cathedral awe and hush-in-the-close. But if it's a house-full day at the Test match or a grand one-dayer, and the sun's in its shirtsleeves on high over Trott's turret, and the cricket down there is tangy and taut, well, you can relish Lord's as the very tangible and cultural epicentre of contented civilisation itself.

Photograph: Laurence Griffiths

Photograph: Stu Fo

Photograph: Adrian Murrell

(top left) Old Trafford, Manchester during the World Cup, India v. Pakistan, June 1999.

(bottom left) Trent Bridge, Nottingham showing Zimbabwe v. England in the World Cup, May 1999.

(top right) The Oval, London.

Photograph: Adrian Murrell

Some of England's county grounds.

(top left) Worcester.

(bottom left) The old Durham ground at Durham University.

(bottom centre) Arundel, Sussex.

(bottom right) Taunton, Somerset.

Photograph: Chris Cole

Photograph: Anton Want

Photograph: Ben Radford

Photograph: Clive Mason

Photograph: Mike Hev

Photograph: Mike Hewitt

South Africa

(top left) The first first-class match played at Soweto, October 1995.

(bottom left) Johannesburg during the Test against India in 1992.

(top right) South Africa v. England in the Sixth One-Day match at the East London ground, January 1996.

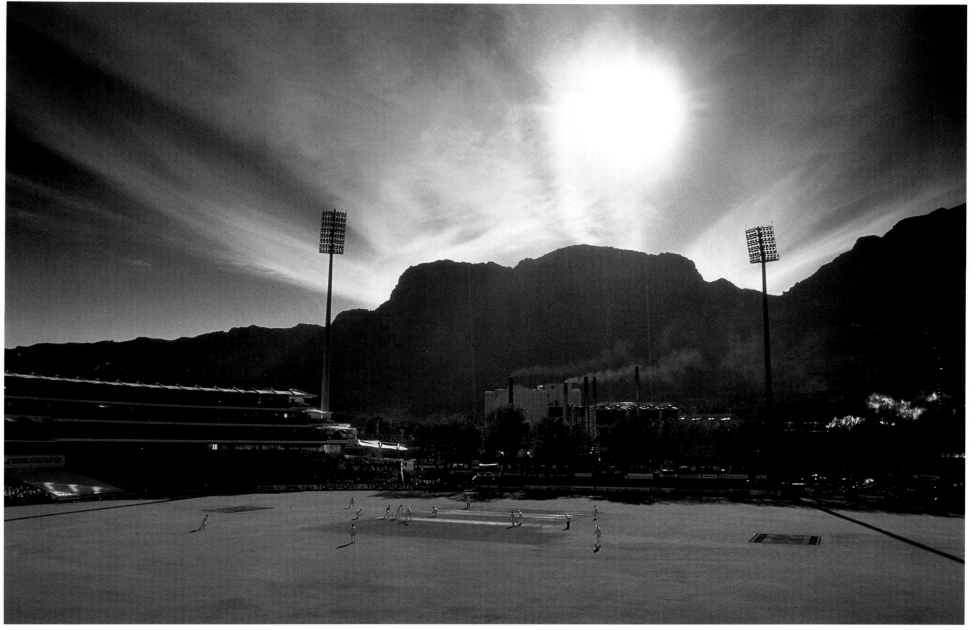

The Newlands ground in Cape Town, South Africa, 1994.

India

Vishakapatnam

Groundstaff erect the shades before a one-day match between Australia and Kenya in the 1996 World Cup.

The match in progress.
Australia v. Kenya in the World Cup, 1996.

Photograph: Adrian Murrell

Photograph: Clive Mason

Photograph: Craig Prentis

Photograph: Craig Prentis

(top left) Bombay   (top right) Delhi   (bottom left) Calcutta   (bottom right) Madras

Photograph: Stu Forster

Photograph: Graham Chad

Photograph: Adrian Murrell

Photograph: Ben Ra

Australia

(top left) Hobart   (top right) Perth   (bottom left) Sydney at night   (bottom right) Adelaide

The First Test between Australia and England at the Gabba, Brisbane, in November 1998
was ended by a massive storm.

The Fourth Test between Australia and England in December 1998 was played at the
Melbourne Cricket Ground.

Sri Lanka

Kurunegala

Pakistan

Karachi

Photograph: Graham Chadwick

Photograph: Graham Chadw

Photograph: Graham Chadwick

New Zealand

The England tour of New Zealand in January 1997.

(top left) Hamilton

(top right) New Plymouth

(bottom left) Palmerston North

West Indies

Antiguans are fanatical about cricket.
Everybody wants to watch or play.

St Vincent from the camera room.

The scoreboard reads:

WEST INDIES	BATTING	AUSTRALIA
CAMPBELL	NO.	TAYLOR
SAMUELS	NO. 6	SLATER
SEMPLE	EXTRAS	BLEWETT
JOSEPH	TOTAL	LANGER
RAGOONATH	WICKET	WAUGH
BROWNE		BOON
DRAKES		WAUGH M
PERRY		HEALY
ANTHONY	BOWLING	REIFFEL
DYSON		MAY
RAMNARINE		

St. Kitts during the Australian tour to the West Indies in 1995.

(opposite) Brian Lara in classic

Chapter Seven

Photograph: Ben Radford

Great Players and Personalities

Photograph: Allsport

Ian Botham during his brilliant innings of 138 for England against Australia in the First Test at Brisbane in November 1986.

Ian Botham beats the then world record for Test dismissals, England v. New Zealand at The Oval in 1986.

Photograph: Allsport / Hulton Getty

(top left) Fred Trueman - Yorkshire and
England, May 1953.

(top right) Colin Milburn - England v.
Australia at Lord's in 1968.

(bottom left) Don Bradman in 1934.

(bottom right) W.G. Grace.

Photograph: Allsport / Hulton Getty

Photograph: Allsport / Hulton Getty

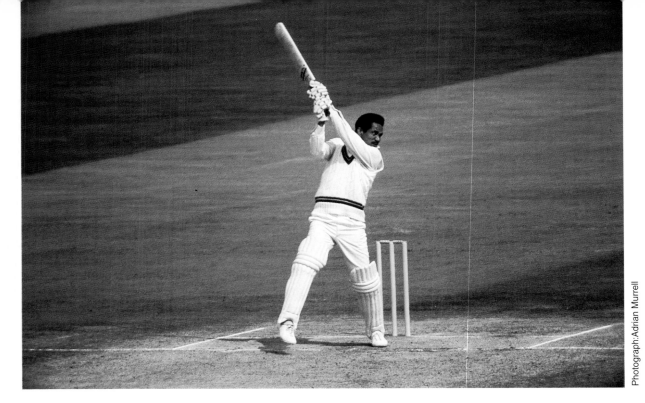

Photograph:Adrian Murrell

Sir Garfield Sobers

Photograph:Allsport

Photograph: Ben Radford

Imran Khan, Pakistan captain playing against India in 1989.

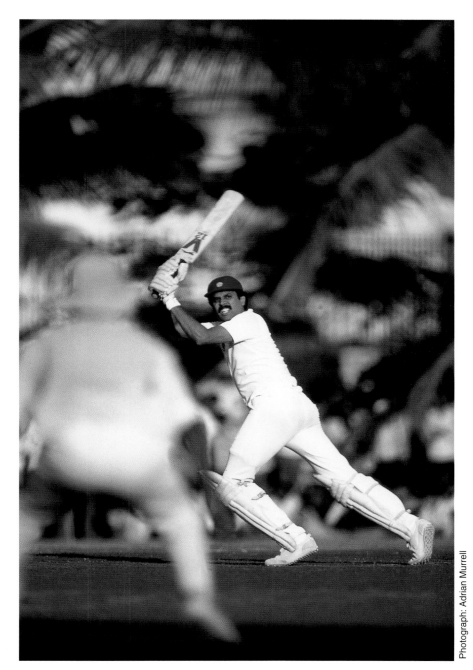

Photograph: Adrian Murrell

Kapil Dev, Indian captain playing in the Second Test against England in Delhi, 1984.

Photograph: Adrian Murrell

Tony Greig, World XI captain v. Australia during Kerry Packer's World Series Cricket in February 1979.

Richard Hadlee of New Zealand, playing against India at Bangalore, November 1986.

Photograph: Simon Bruty

Photograph: Adrian Murrell

Rodney Marsh, the great Australian wicket-keeper, during an Australian tour match v. Hampshire in August 1980.

Photograph: Allsport

Bob Taylor, England wicket-keeper.

Alan Knott, Kent and England wicket-keeper.

Photograph: Adrian Murrell

Jeff Dujon takes the ball in the Second One-Day match against England at Old Trafford, Manchester.

Photograph: Bob Martin

Photograph: Allsport

Dennis Lillee.

Jeff Thomson.

Civilisation Under the Sun

Context is all

Those great innings were not one-off 'played for' manifestations - like a 100-metre 'record attempt' at athletics. They emerged from the context of the match, the state of the game. Does not Lara himself, for instance, tell you that his matchwinning single hundred against Australia in the very last year of the century was far, far more rewarding than his two obliterating record-breakers? For context and the 'team game' is all. Anyway, does it even have to be a three-figure score to be the grandest of all? What about Victor Trumper's 74 (out of 122) in 1904? Or Dexter's 70 at Lord's in 1963? Or Gower's 72 in Perth in 1982? Or Eddie Paynter's 83 at Brisbane in 1933? Was Hutton's apparently sublime 37 at Sydney in 1946 actually finer than his record marathon at The Oval eight years before? I daresay it was. Was Graeme Pollock's 125 at Trent Bridge in 1965 the most glorious innings ever by a left-hander, Lara and Sobers included? It might well have been. Or was it one by Neil Harvey or David Gower or Martin Donnelly? Will Botham's 'unforgettable' 149 at Leeds in his annus mirabilis of 1981 be forgotten by history as less dramatically the genuine article than his 118 in the same series at Manchester? I think so, others don't. Were innings by West Indian feast-founder George Headley (106 out of 277, and 107 out of 225) against England at Lord's in 1939 the two greatest successive Test innings ever played? Probably. Was Sobers' counterattacking 132 which set up the astonishing tie at Brisbane in 1961 better than Viv Richards' 56-ball century in Antigua in 1986? Who knows? Were the great Compton's 145 and 184 better than Randall's 174 and 150 in 1977-78? And were either of those better than Gooch's 333 at Lord's, or his 154 out of 231 at Headingley? And what about Jessop, and Hobbs, and McCabe, and Greenidge, and Jayasuriya, and Tendulkar, and Merchant, and Javed Miandad . . . Where stands now Willie Watson at Lord's in 1953 and, for that matter, Michael Atherton at Johannesburg in 1995? On and on we could go - and, anyway, what about all those gallant stands and blazing innings, and matchwinning catches which were witnessed and hurrahed, but never logged for posterity, all down those aeons of sunlit days even before cricket was first called cricket at Hambledon . . . ? For,

> 'Patient, dramatic, serious, genial,
> From over to over the game goes on.
> Weaving its pattern of hardy perennial
> Civilisation under the sun.'

Hey, I've just looked it up: Gerald William Bullett's lovely poem was first published in October, 1937. The month that I was born.

Photograph: Adrian Murrell

Bob Willis, English fast bowler, in the Fourth Test against India in January 1982.

Joel Garner, Somerset and West Indies fast bowler, 1983.

Andy Roberts, West Indies fast bowler, 1976.

Michael Holding (West Indies) bowls to Mike Brearley (England captain) during a One-Day match in Sydney, Australia, 1979.

Colin Croft, top West Indies bowler in the Second Test against India at Faisalabad in 1980.

Malcolm Marshall, bowling for the West Indies, who beat Australia in the Benson and Hedges One-Day final, Sydney, January 1989.

Merv Hughes (Australia) appeals for the wicket of Andy Caddick in the First Test, England v. Australia at Old Trafford in June 1993.

Photograph: Mike Hewitt

Craig McDermott, Australian fast bowler, in the First Test v. South Africa, Johannesburg, March 1994.

Photograph: Clive Mason

Glenn McGrath (Australia) in the Fourth Test against England at Headingley, July 1997.

Photograph:Adrian Murrell

Curtly Ambrose (West Indies) clean-bowls Darren Gough (England) in the Second Test at Lord's in 1995.

Courtney Walsh celebrates the West Indies' victory over Australia by one run in the Fourth Test at Adelaide, January 1993.

Photograph: Joe Mann

(above) **South Africa's Allan Donald in action:**

(left) against England in the Second One-Day International at Old Trafford, Manchester, August 1994.

(right) in a One-Day International against Zimbabwe at Harare, October 1995.

(below right) Shaun Pollock (South Africa) during a tour match against the Duke of Norfolk's XI in 1998.

Australia's Shane Warne in action:

(below) bowling to Graham Thorpe in the Third Test against England at Old Trafford in July 1997.

(right) celebrating a wicket in the World Cup against South Africa in 1999.

Photograph: Graham Chadwick

Anil Kumble, India v. Nottinghamshire in a World Cup warm-up match, May 1999.

Photograph: Clive Mason

Muttiah Muralitharan (Sri Lanka) bowls to Mark Waugh (Australia) in the Carlton & United One-Day series, Australia, January 1999.

Photograph: Craig Prentis

Wasim Akram, Pakistan's captain in the 1999 World Cup.

England v. Australia, the Second Test at Lord's in June 1997. Rival captains Mike Atherton (England) and Mark Taylor (Australia) share a joke.

Photograph: Clive Mason

Photograph: Graham Chadwick

Mike Atherton in pensive mood during England's tour match against New Zealand 'A' at Wanganui in February 1997.

Photograph:Adrian Murrell

Graham Gooch during his historic innings of 333 against India in the First Test at Lord's in 1990.

Photograph:Ben Radford

Graham Gooch and Mike Gatting talk tactics over net practice during England's tour of India in 1993.

Photograph: Adrian Murrell

Sunil Gavaskar (India) batting against Zimbabwe in the 1987 World Cup at Bombay.

Photograph: Ben Radford

West Indies openers Gordon Greenidge and Desmond Haynes (standing) in the Fifth Test against England, Antigua, February 1990.

Geoff Boycott during his 100th century, England v.
Australia at Headingley in 1977.

Geoff Boycott (Yorkshire and England) during a Sunday League match,
Yorkshire v. Gloucestershire in August 1983.

Photograph: Adrian Murrell

Photograph: Shaun Botterill

Photograph: Ben Radford

Arjuna Ranatunga - Sri Lanka.

Michael Slater - Australia.

Gary Kirsten - South Africa.

Photograph: Graham Chadwick

(above) West Indies' Richie Richardson batting for the Leeward Islands v. England, January 1990.

(top right) Salim Malik - Pakistan.

(bottom right) Javed Miandad of Pakistan in the Third Test v. England at Old Trafford, June 1992.

Greg Chappell - Australia.

Ian Chappell - Australia.

Australian captain Steve Waugh (left) with twin brother Mark.

Photograph: Ben Radford

Steve Waugh in action.

Photograph: Craig Prentis

Photograph: Ben Radford

David Gower at the Melvista Oval, Australia, 1990.

David Gower and Mike Gatting, 1985.

Photograph: Adrian Murrell

David Boon - Australia.

Allan Border - Australian captain.

Photograph: Adrian Murrell

Allan Lamb - England.

Photograph: Graham Chadwick

Nasser Hussain of England, reaches 100 in the
Sixth Test v. West Indies in Antigua, 1998.

Photograph: Stu Forster

Photograph: Adrian Murrell

Graeme Hick - England.

Graeme Hick and Alec Stewart.

Photograph: Adrian Murrell

Clive Lloyd - West Indies.

Photograph: Adrian Murrell

Martin Crowe - New Zealand.

Viv Richards - West Indies.

Photograph:Adrian Murrell

Photograph:Ben Radford

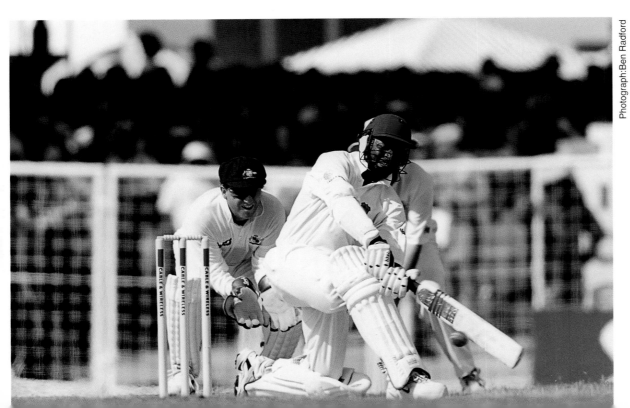

Brian Lara - West Indies captain.

Sachin Tendulkar - India.

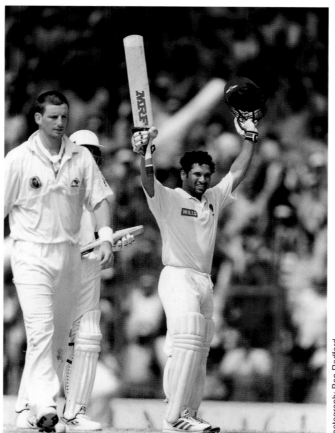

Photograph: Ben Radford

Photograph: Adrian Murrell

(clockwise from above)
Hansie Cronje - South Africa,
Alvin Kallicharran - West Indies,
Barry Richards - South Africa,
Mushtaq Mohammad - Pakistan.

Photograph: Allsport

RUMBELOWS   AA 01-
                  21

Photograph: Adrian Murrell

Darren Gough (left) and Mark Butcher celebrate England's exciting victory
over Australia in the Fourth Test at Melbourne in December 1998.